Unusual Pets

MINI PIGS

MARYSA STORM

BLACK RABBIT BOOKS

Bolt is published by Black Rabbit Books
P.O. Box 227, Mankato, Minnesota, 56002.
www.blackrabbitbooks.com

Alissa Thielges, editor; Rhea Magaro, designer and photo researcher

Library of Congress Cataloging-in-Publication Data
Names: Storm, Marysa, author.
Title: Mini pigs / by Marysa Storm.
Description: Mankato, MN: Black Rabbit Books, [2026] | Series: Unusual pets | Includes bibliographical references and index. | Audience: Ages 8–12 | Audience: Grades 4–6
Identifiers: LCCN 2024043407 (print) | LCCN 2024043408 (ebook) | ISBN 9781644667804 (library binding) | ISBN 9781644667927 (ebook)
Subjects: LCSH: Miniature pigs—Juvenile literature. | Swine—Juvenile literature.
Classification: LCC SF393.M55 S765 2026 (print) | LCC SF393.M55 (ebook) | DDC 636.4/0887—dc23/eng/20250109
LC record available at https://lccn.loc.gov/2024043407

Image Credits

Alamy Stock Photo/Arco Images / Steimer, C., 4–5, Tierfotoagentur / R. Richter, 31; Dreamstime/Cynoclub, 3, Hanna Yeremyeyeva, 32, Ingugulija, 23; Shutterstock/andreyphoto63, 25, Chase D'animulls, 28–29, cynoclub, 15 (top), 24, Danz Abilizza, 22, Daria Miroshnikova, 23, Eric Isselee, 15 (bottom), Formatoriginal, 25, Goodwyn Ferrell, 22–23, Jamilya13, 1, Joe Herlong, 11 (top), Kritchai7752, 25, Kseniia Derzhavina, 22, Lei Luke, 18, Linn Currie, 8, M. Unal Ozmen, 25, Macrovector, 26, Manee_Meena, 25, Martin Bergsma, 21, MENSAH DE-ANGELO SHAKUR, cover, NIKCOA, 25, Photodigitaal.nl, 11 (bottom), Plotitsyna NiNa, 10, Rita_Kochmarjova, 13, 27, Robyn Mackenzie, 25, Sanit Fuangnakhon, 16–17, Shirelady, 6–7, Tim UR, 25, Tiny Turkey, 22, Ton Bangkeaw, 9
Every effort has been made to contact copyright holders for material reproduced in this book. Any omissions will be rectified in subsequent printings if notice is given to the publisher.

CONTENTS

CHAPTER 1

Meet the MINI PIG

The little pig eats and eats. Once the food is all gone, it snorts at its owner. The boy laughs. "You had plenty!" The little pig snorts again. "Okay, but you'll have to work for it." The young boy gathers some food from the fridge. Then, he leads his pig into the backyard.

Play Time!

Outside, a small plastic pool is filled with water. The boy drops the food into the pool. Pieces of lettuce float. Other food sinks to the bottom. The pig makes an excited barking noise. Then it charges toward the pool. Splash! What fun!

Not everyone can keep a mini pig. It's important to check local laws before adopting one.

CHAPTER 2

A SPECIAL PET

Mini pigs are special pets, but they aren't a special **species** of pig. Instead, they're normal pigs **bred** to be small. Owners must make sure to get their mini pigs from trustworthy breeders. If not, their little pigs may someday become quite large!

Mini pigs are also called teacup pigs and micro pigs.

Vietnamese pot-bellied pig

Juliana mini pig

Kunekune mini pig

Smart and Friendly

Mini pigs, like other pigs, are smart animals. They can be taught tricks and be potty trained. They are friendly too. Many mini pigs like to cuddle. Some mini pigs can be kept with other pets. They can get along well with friendly cats and dogs. They do best with other pigs though.

In the United States, mini pigs became popular pets in the

1990s.

CHAPTER 3

Mini Pig FEATURES

Mini pigs have **snouts**, short legs, and hooves. Their thick skin has stiff hairs. Like all pigs, mini pigs can't sweat. But they can get sunburn.

A mini pig is not "mini" in size. It is smaller than a regular pig, but it still weighs a lot. It can grow bigger than a large dog. To know how big a piglet will get, look at the pig's parents. The piglet will grow to a similar size.

COMPARING SIZES

MINI PIG

REGULAR PIG

PARTS OF A MINI PIG

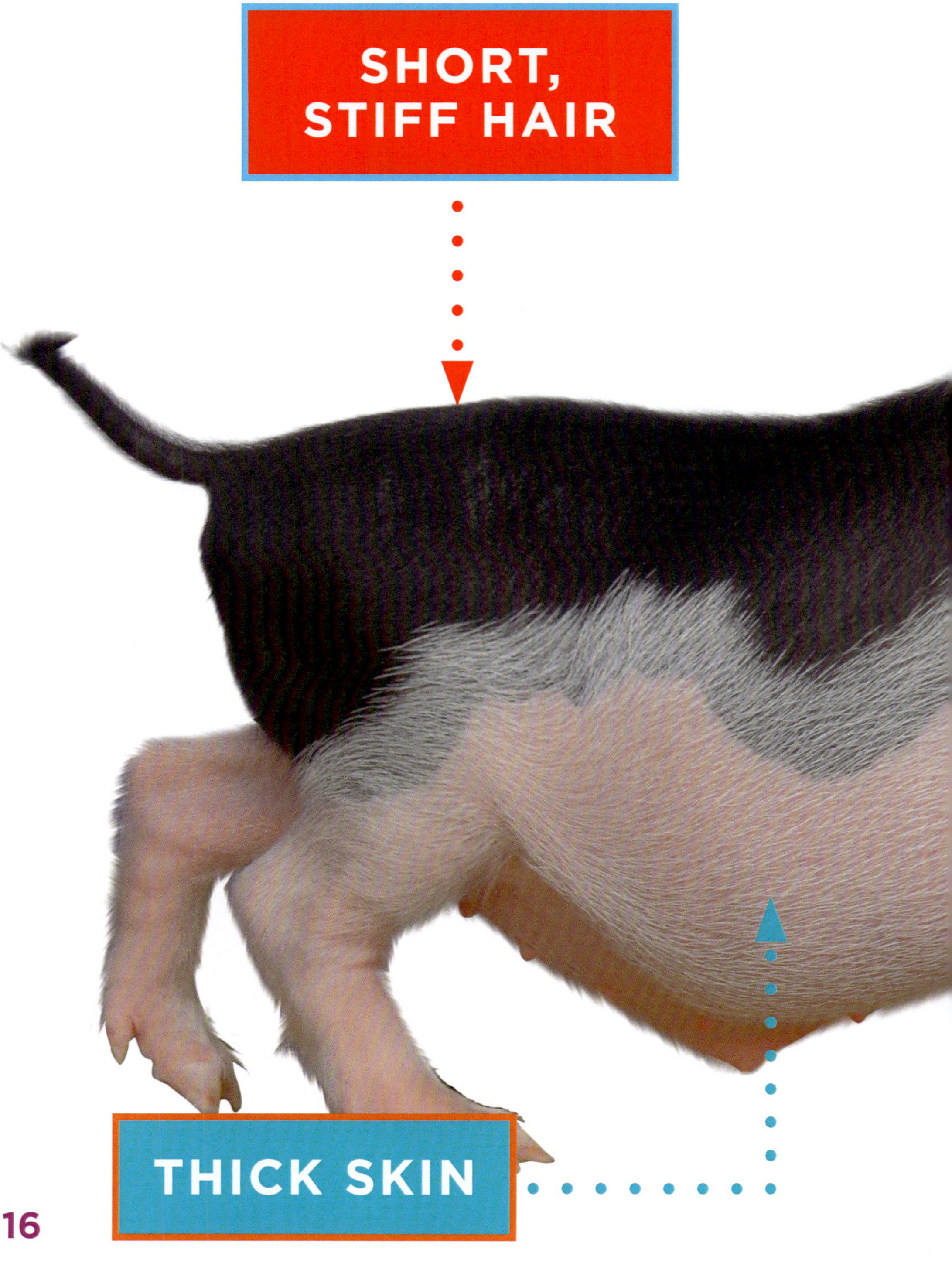

FLOPPY EARS
SNOUT
HOOVES

Super Snout

Mini pigs have a great sense of smell. In fact, they can smell as well as some dogs. Pigs can even smell things underground. If they smell something tasty, they'll **root** for it. Mini pigs might leave their owners' yards looking a little rough.

Pigs can not see well.

CHAPTER 4

Caring for a MINI PIG

Mini pigs can be kept outside or indoors. When outside, they need a place to sleep with straw bedding. Shelter from the sun is important too. If inside, they need a large litter box and a soft spot to sleep. It's important that pigs have time to root around and **forage**.

Pigs are smart. They like toys and games.

WHAT THEY NEED

soft spot to sleep

litter box (if inside)

toys

shelter from the sun (when outside)
fresh water

Food for Thought

If they could, pigs would eat all day! Owners need to make sure they don't overfeed their mini pigs. They need to keep anything their pigs might eat locked up. To be safe, anything **toxic** should be kept away too. Pigs need regular walks too. This keeps them in shape.

WHAT CAN MINI PIGS EAT?

GOOD FOODS ✓

Pig pellets

Fresh vegetables

Grains

Fresh fruit

BAD FOODS X

Most fruit seeds and pits

Uncooked beans

Salt

Meat and fish

A Happy Home

Mini pigs need special care. Their hooves need trimming about every six months. Since mini pigs can't sweat, it's important they don't get too hot. If outside, they need a shady spot. A **shallow** pool to play in is good too. Good owners are mindful of their pig's every need.

PERFECT TEMP

60 to 76 degrees Fahrenheit (16 to 24 degrees Celsius)

By the NUMBERS

4 to 5 years

AGE WHEN MINI PIGS ARE FULLY GROWN

more than

$1,000

HOW MUCH IT COSTS TO BUY A MINI PIG

20

NUMBER OF DIFFERENT SOUNDS A PIG CAN MAKE

15 to 18 YEARS

HOW LONG MINI PIGS LIVE

GLOSSARY

bred (BREHD)—having two specific animals mate to create young with certain characteristics

forage (FAWR-ij)—to search for something

root (ROOT)—to look for food under the ground by digging with the nose

shallow (SHAL-oh)—having a small distance to the bottom from the surface

snout (SNOUT)—the projecting part of an animal's face that includes the nose or nose and mouth

species (SPEE-seez)—a class of individuals that have common characteristics and share a common name

toxic (TOK-sik)—poisonous

BOOKS

Herschbach, Elizabeth. *Small Mammals*. Minneapolis: Abdo Publishing Company, 2024.

Leatherland, Noah. *Life Cycle of a Pig*. Minneapolis: Bearport Publishing Company, 2025.

Polinsky, Paige V. *My Pet Mini Pig*. Minneapolis: Bellwether Media, 2020.

WEBSITES

General Facts about Mini-Pigs
vcahospitals.com/know-your-pet/general-facts-about-mini-pigs

Mini Pig Facts and Myths
americanminipigassociation.com/owners/ready-mini-pig-owner/mini-pig-facts-myths/

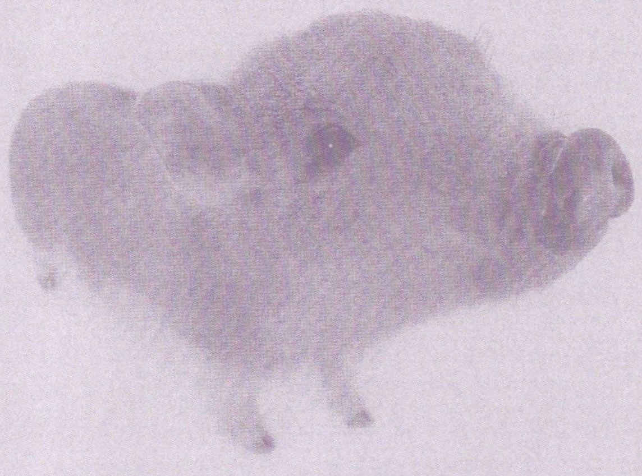

INDEX

BOOKS

Herschbach, Elizabeth. *Small Mammals*. Minneapolis: Abdo Publishing Company, 2024.

Leatherland, Noah. *Life Cycle of a Pig*. Minneapolis: Bearport Publishing Company, 2025.

Polinsky, Paige V. *My Pet Mini Pig*. Minneapolis: Bellwether Media, 2020.

WEBSITES

General Facts about Mini-Pigs
vcahospitals.com/know-your-pet/general-facts-about-mini-pigs

Mini Pig Facts and Myths
americanminipigassociation.com/owners/ready-mini-pig-owner/mini-pig-facts-myths/

INDEX